GRANDMA'S BASICS SEWING

POCKET GUIDE TO LEARN SEWING WITH BASIC INFORMATION AND TECHNIQUES TO EASILY REPAIR YOUR CLOTHES!

ELEANOR NELSON

CONTENTS

Introduction v

1. Sewing, the Start 1
2. Sewing Machine Basics 7
3. What Types of Sewing Exist? 14
4. Tools 22
5. Basic Sewing Patterns 42

Conclusions 79

© **Copyright 2021 by Eleanor Nelson- All rights reserved**.

This document is geared towards providing exact and reliable information in regard to the topic and issue covered.

- From a Declaration of Principles which was accepted and approved equally by a Committee of the American Bar Association and a Committee of Publishers and Associations.

In no way is it legal to reproduce, duplicate, or transmit any part of this document in either electronic means or in printed format. All rights reserved.

The information provided herein is stated to be truthful and consistent, in that any liability, in terms of inattention or otherwise, by any usage or abuse of any policies, processes, or directions contained within is the solitary and utter responsibility of the recipient reader. Under no circumstances will any legal responsibility or blame be held against the publisher for any reparation, damages, or monetary loss due to the information herein, either directly or indirectly.

Respective authors own all copyrights not held by the publisher.

The information herein is offered for informational purposes solely and is universal as so. The presentation of the information is without contract or any type of guaranteed assurance.

The trademarks that are used are without any consent, and the publication of the trademark is without permission or backing by the trademark owner. All trademarks and brands within this book are for clarifying purposes only and are owned by the owners themselves, not affiliated with this document.

❦ Created with Vellum

INTRODUCTION

Sewing is quickly becoming one of the worlds' most popular crafts again. The rise in the cost of living and the average drop or stagnation of wages means we can't always afford to go out and buy what we want. Whipping up a dress, skirt, or even a t-shirt that looks like it came out of an expensive boutique is not difficult if you concentrate and put your mind to it. As you have seen, it is better to learn how to sew using both a machine and by hand as you can use a combination of the two skills when making your creations.

All the topics covered in the book are truly meant for helping our readers in establishing a firm practice about the art of sewing. So you need to give a look at all these chapters so that any critical chapter cannot be overlooked.

But the direct explanation increases the speed

INTRODUCTION

throughout the following chapters. The basis of starting with the introductory information is very logical. It is projected to set up all the readers completely familiar with the thought of the topic.

The book starts with a brief but elaborative note about the basic concepts of sewing. So all you need is to first grab all these concepts and then move on to learning the practical features. The concepts are mentioned in a way that will be beneficial to apply in the practical aspect of sewing. The discussion then extends to the sewing tools and devices, so that the reader can easily apply the concepts in judging the right type of tool.

SEWING, THE START

Sewing is the art of sewing a fabric with a needle and thread, which humans first discovered in the Paleolithic era. History also dates it to the same period when prehistoric technological roots in human evolution took shape. For some people, the talent of sewing is innate because they saw their mothers or friends sewing. It may seem a little intimidating at first; however, the truth is, with zillions of sewing types, styles, and options, you will soon find one that suits your interests! Often, it's good for a beginner to start with hand sewing, as it prepares the mind for the hands-on process of how sewing happens. While hand sewing itself has its versions of continuous stitching and embroidery, there are superb sewing machines and accessories to reduce the fatigue you experience while sewing for hours manually with your hands!

Whether you are a sewing idiot or a returning sewing student, this is an art with overwhelming creativity. It generates the patience, beauty, and skill for complexity in every person. Sewing is not just for tailors because from sewing pillowcases to beautiful bedspreads, there are zillions of sewing options to fit whatever your comfort zone is. Sewing is one of the best-voted hobbies suitable for all ages as it is also therapeutic.

Sewing is a skill that traditionally only women and homemakers learned. Today so much has changed, and everyone wants to learn as many essential skills as possible if it means they can improve their lives. Sewing is a great skill to master because of its many benefits, not only to repair clothes quickly but also to enjoy the fun involved in exploring creativity and creating new garments.

Reasons to Start Sewing

Regardless of what you want to do with your finished results and in addition to having the skills necessary to complete any project that catches your eye, you can also:
- Improve hand-eye coordination

- Learn how to blend color and create art or decorations in a very different medium
- Copy expensive or designer clothing or costumes for less money
- Start a small side business making crafts, purses, clothes, or accessories
- Express yourself through the fabric
- Have something to do with your hands during downtime
- Learn a relaxing skill that keeps your hands busy while your mind is clear

Most importantly, you'll learn a new skill that can challenge you and give you a great sense of accomplishment. After all, there's nothing like finishing a project like a new skirt and trying it on for the first time or completing a new set of curtains or a new slipcover that can transform a room in your home in minutes.

Sewing is also a skill that will help you save money, as buying clothes can be quite expensive. You can also count on the therapeutic nature of sewing, as you start a task with odds and ends that don't go well together and end the task with a garment that looks brilliant. I have a few other reasons why you might want to explore couture.

To explore **your independence**

When you can make your clothes, you can enjoy a

certain level of independence. If you need to attend a function or need a special outfit on short notice, you are not limited to looking for an open store or somewhere to make a purchase. You can simply create what you want to wear, ensuring that you maintain a unique look at a moment's notice.

Sewing is convenient

Sewing will save you money for making clothes, but there are so many other items you can sew. You can create specialty items that you can use to decorate your home, including curtains and tablecloths, or create a wide range of crafts. With sewing skills, you don't have to worry about buying gifts for others; you can create personalized gifts with ease.

Sewing allows you to create your style

Many people like to have a unique look, a style that stands out and helps identify them as an individual. Being able to sew allows you to define how you want to look, so you never have to worry about looking like someone else when you leave home. If you have clothes you have purchased before, you will find that you can easily alter them to make them fit you better if you have adequate sewing skills.

. . .

Go against stereotypes

Things have changed, and now more men are sewing, as can be seen by the many clothing designers who have shared their collections. Nowadays, sewing is a means to explore your creativity, and gender bias is quickly dissipating.

Sewing helps protect the environment

Being able to sew gives you the perfect opportunity to reuse materials and create unique items for a wide range of purposes. This saves you from buying new materials or throwing away the ones you have that might be suitable for another item. Things like curtains can easily be converted into pillow covers, and even an old pair of jeans can make an excellent pair of t-shirts with a matching bag. All of this is possible if you know how to sew.

Sewing allows you to replicate

Have you ever seen a fantastic design for a garment on a runway and know that you can't afford to purchase it? You can look at it and get inspiration to create a similar garment if you know how to sew. Also, many clothes are made in generic sizes for models but may not be ideal for the actual person who is meant to wear the item. When you know how to sew, you can make sure that you create a garment that fits well on your entire body so that you can make the most of your physique.

SEWING IS **great**

Once you have completed a sewing project that you have worked on, you will feel accomplished and feel good about your work. What would be even better is wearing your item in public and receiving some praise for it. Because sewing is a skill, you will only improve with more practice and the passage of time, and before you realize it., you will be able to create with confidence any item you require as long as you have access to a needle and thread.

SEWING SKILLS WILL ALWAYS BE **relevant**

No matter where you may be in the world, and whatever your social standing, knowing how to sew will always be an asset. This is because people worldwide need clothes to cover their bodies, and they can also use these skills to earn income.

SEWING MACHINE BASICS

Types of Machines

Blue/Cantor/Q Needle

This machine uses a stretch needlepoint type and is best used to prevent snagging and skipped stitches. This also works best for microfibers and knits, among other fabrics.

European 130/705HJ

This machine uses the Tightly Woven Fabric system and works best for upholstery, denim, and heavier types of corduroy.

American 15 x 1DE

These have sharp needles and are best used for sewing jeans, denim, and other heavy fabrics.

American 130/705H or 15 x 1DE

This is ideal for beginners, as it is a universal sewing machine and works for most thread types and fabrics.

. . .

Selection by Functionality

Straight Nose Sewing Machine

They can sew with one, two, or three needles. They make closed seams.

Overlock machine

This is also known as an overlock. You can make an overcast stitch, preventing the selvages from fraying.

Overlock machine

The seam on this machine is flat and is ideal for knitting. You can do topstitching and also closed stitching.

Collar machine

The ribbon is fed through a funnel, which is folded for parts of the fabric with curved areas such as the collar of a shirt.

Bastera Machine

Creates invisible stitches that are used for hems or hemming in skirts and pants.

Docking machine

It is used in places where fabric is subjected to a lot of stretching. Secure pockets.

Button machine

Glues flat buttons together in all sorts of ways.

Creates cups and can cut them automatically.

Closure Machine

It makes a chain stitch with a French stitch and is

used to close pants, sleeves, and shirts, among other things.

Elastic Machine

Applies elastic bands.

Cutting machine

Cuts according to a pattern and the depth of a blade.

Sewing Machine Composition

Reverse Lever

Also known as a reverse button. This is used to finish seams. For some seams, it is customary to reinforce the stitches with reverse seams.

This ensures the strength and total finish of the manufactured pieces. This is a very convenient use, especially when you start sewing and when you want to ensure the quality of clothing.

Graduation wheel

This corresponds to the wheel located on the side of the machine. This wheel is rotated and allows you to pierce or remove the needle from the fabric. It is usually handy when the needle is stuck and needs to be removed manually.

Sometimes you can use the roulette wheel to start working the machine instead of using the foot pedal. This process is considered much slower but is certainly safer.

Coil holder

This is where the wire is located and is also known as wire tension. Depending on the thickness of the wire, the small wire needs to be adjusted, ranging from 0 to 9. Number 4 is considered normal; however, if we are dealing with the thicker or thinner thread, it requires adjustment.

Presser's foot

After placing the thread in the machine, you will find the presser foot. This can be operated through a small lever generally located at the back of the machine. If you want to thread the needle, you'll need to raise it; you'll need to lower it to start sewing.

Stitch selection buttons

These knobs let you adjust the width and length of the mesh. To do this, you must choose the number according to your needs. If you wish to tighten the seam, you can use zero (0); You'll do multiple stitches in one spot with this number. However, if you would like to create short dots, use the number 1 (for example, a buttonhole). The number 2 is considered normal, and numbers higher than twox2 are used for basting seams.

Sewing plate

This is the base where the presser foot and needle are located. The drive teeth are also located in this area.

Spool holder

This is a small metal drawer that is easily removable. Inside is the bobbin and thread.

FAQ

What purpose will my sewing machine serve?

Do you want a machine to sew your clothes, sew your neighbors' clothes, and do some work, or do you want to engage professionally in sewing? Choosing a machine with motor power depends on the goal the sewing machine will accomplish. You can check the machine's features and even look directly at the datasheet on the manufacturer's page. If you are already a professional and the goal is industrial sewing, don't worry; many workshop machines are great second-hand and at reasonable prices.

What level of sewing am I at?

If it's the first sewing machine you've ever bought, it's best to buy a machine that's neither too expensive nor too complex because when you're starting, you don't know if you're going to like it or you just don't know if it's going to work well for you. Also, just because it's a cheap machine doesn't mean it's terrible. Suppose you're already at that stage where you've been sewing with machines since the year your mother was born, and despite the difficulties of being an old machine, you're good at sewing with it. In that case, I recommend buying a good quality machine, but not overly expensive. If you are already at a very advanced level, indeed you have already tried several brands, and you know more or less the brand that suits you best and the advantages you want the machine to have for the jobs you usually do.

Mechanical or electric?

Well, here it will depend on taste and how well you know the technology. Mechanical machines are simple: no screens, no stories, just wheels, but perhaps lack the advantages of making programmed or embroidered trapdoor mallets. On the other hand, the electric ones are of a higher range, most with a touch screen, and tend to have more functionality.

expensive.

Whatever I have to do if I get caught in the middle of two similar models?

I will choose the last model if the brand is the same. If it's two different brands, it's a matter of taste. I'm more of a singer person, but some people prefer Alfa. If you are in doubt, I would look at the motor's power, as this has a significant influence on the ability to sew fabrics together, as well as denim and elastic, and ensure that the strength of the fabric is better and does not hit the jumps.

Was the translation helpful?

Which brand should I choose?

I always say the same thing, but for me, these are the best and guarantee quality: Alfa and Singer are my favorites. Brother is not bad either, or JUKI is the best if you want a good machine but a little more

Tips:

- For a sewing machine to be considered old, its manufacturing date must be before 1900. So, check its history and model, as well as they will help you to certify the age of the machine.

- Take a close look at the materials it is made of and the condition it is in. Check the level of deterioration or wear of the mechanical parts, the paint, and the cabinet or drawer in which it is stored.

- Examine the accessories and see if it has the original wooden box, manual, keys, and paperwork. These items increase the price of the machine.

Make sure your supplier can service it with quality parts. Also, find accessories that can help you always keep your old sewing machine in good condition.

WHAT TYPES OF SEWING EXIST?

One of the reasons that sewing is such a broad type of hobby to learn is that there are so many different kinds. And many of these types have subcategories that can branch out in seemingly endless ways, such as the many different kinds of cross stitch or the multiple types of embroidery stitches that you can learn.

This basic overview of sewing types will help you get an understanding of what they are, as well as for when you may want to use them.

MACHINE SEWING

Sewing by machine is a lot faster than attempting the same project by hand, which is why so many people want to learn how to use a sewing machine and figure out what it can do. Your basic sewing machine has a lot of functions. It can:

- Sew straight or curved lines with stitches of varying lengths
- Make zig-zag stitches of different sizes and length
- Make loose basting-style stitches that can hold things together temporarily while you put in more decorative stitching later

Depending on your machine, you may also be able to make decorative topstitching and embroidery as well. And while a standard sewing machine doesn't seem as though it has that many functions, you can use those few functions in a variety of ways to get the finished piece you're after.

For example, a sewing machine can:

- Sew two pieces of fabric together near the edge to form a hem
- Piece together several smaller sections of fabric, such as a quilt block
- Zig-zag stitch the raw edges of the fabric to help prevent them from fraying over time
- Applique thin pieces of fabric onto another section of fabric by either straight sewing or zig-zag stitching the edges

And when you stop to think about all the many projects that just quickly stitching multiple pieces of fabric together can make, your sewing machine can quickly become your best friend.

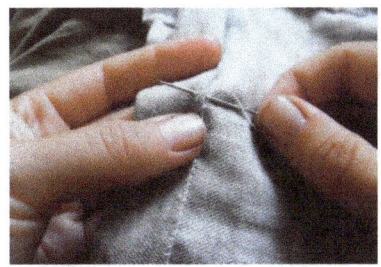

HAND SEWING

Even if you decide that you want to make most of your projects by machine, you should still learn a few basic stitches by hand. Why? Some projects may need you to finish a small section by hand, or you may find yourself far from home with a hem that's suddenly fallen and no machine to help tack it up. You can also stitch by hand anywhere from the office, school, the park—bringing along your sewing machine is a lot more awkward and cumbersome than just bringing a needle and some thread.

Stitching by hand also gives you a lot more options than your machine does. Remember, unless you've purchased a fancy machine that can do embroidery and decorative stitching, you're only going to get things like that if you stitch them up by hand.

Using basic hand stitches, you can:

- Sew a hem
- Tack up a hem to machine sew later
- Piece together multiple pieces of small fabric, such as a quilt block
- Blanket stitch two edges together, such as craft felt, to make a unique design or applique
- Make decorative applique stitches using embroidery thread

- Embroider names, designs and varying colors into clothing
- Cross stitch a design for display or for use on clothing

And this is just the start. Machines make things easy and fast to put together, but they have limitations. Hand stitching lets you make all the same things, plus multiple others with a lot of different decorative stitches at the same time. So when you're learning how to sew, you should take the time to learn at least a few different types of hand stitching at the same time, so you can expand your productivity later.

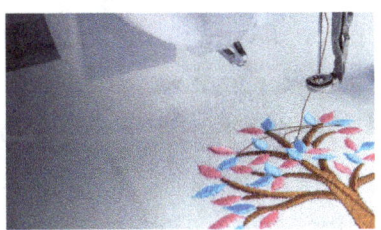

EMBROIDERY

If you want to put your own personal stamp on anything from tablecloths to clothes, embroidery is the way to do it. Embroidery involves making decorative, colorful patterns and images on cloth using a special heavy thread and various types of stitches. Most embroidery involves a variety of different stitches and colors within a pattern. You can use any type of cloth to embroider, and you can also embroider using some specialty sewing machines.

Embroidery can be a fun way to sew your name onto something, stitch the outline of a car onto a toddler's t-shirt, or make a 3-D raised design around the collar of a shirt. Once you've learned some basic hand-sewing stitches, it's easy to make the jump to embroidery by using some of the same stitches as your starting point and placing them where they can be seen, with a thread and needle large enough to give you the look you're after.

Cross-stitching can also be used to decorate fabric, but it differs from embroidery in a few ways. There are several different cross-stitches, but the basic principle remains the same; you make two stitches per square of fabric, with the two stitches crossing or intersecting with one another in some way.

To achieve this, cross-stitching is usually done on fabric that is easily divided into a grid, such as linen. Cross-stitched patterns can take on many different looks, from abstract color to detailed scenes, but they all have a similar geometric look to them based on the grid of the fabric and the nature of the stitches.

Cross-stitching is simple once you get the hang of it, and it can be a relaxing way to add some color and detail to your life. The repetitive nature of the stitches means that you don't have to pay close attention to what you are doing, much like knitting, which makes cross-stitching a great activity for when you're watching TV or waiting for an appointment.

APPLIQUE

Applique is the process of layering pieces of fabric into a pattern. This could be cutting out shapes and attaching them to a shirt, or it could be attaching a decorative border to a set of curtains.

There are several ways you can applique. The most common involves simply stitching around the edge of a shape to attach it to the one below. Depending on what type of fabric you're using, however, this may not be enough, because the fabric edge could either curl or unravel. To fix this, you can either fold the edge of the decorative piece under before stitching it done, or you could use a different type of stitch to help cover the edge of the decorative piece to hold it flat and prevent any unraveling.

Any type of fabric can be used in applique. Felt, jersey knit, cotton; you can get very creative with the applique process joining together multiple shapes and colors. I once appliqued a felt bus onto my son's shirt using embroidery thread and a blanket stitch.

Using applique can let you decorate and personalize nearly anything. And because you can use simple stitches or even a sewing machine to do so, anyone can learn to applique no matter what your level of expertise with a needle and thread.

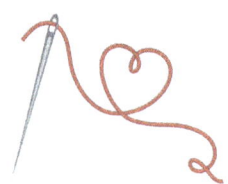

TOOLS

There's no end to the variety of supplies you can have. But before you break the bank, focus on the essentials first. You may already have some tools at home or have some replacement supplies you could use before buying specialized tools.

Here are the essential tools you'll need:

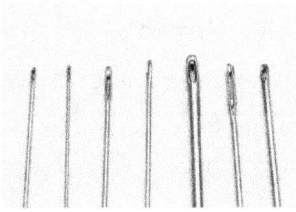

SEWING NEEDLES

Different types of needles are sold for various purposes. Buy a needle set that comes with different types and sizes of needles. This way, you will have the right needle for the type of fabric you want to work with.

THREAD

It is crucial to get good-quality thread for your sewing projects. When choosing the right thread, make sure that the color of the thread is like the fabric you are working with. Also, make sure that the thread has a smooth finish. Avoid fuzzy threads as they can break easily and can produce lint over time.

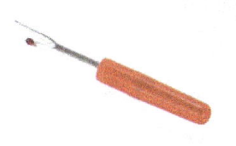

SEAM RIPPER

A sewing splitter is a tool that lets you loosen a faulty stitch so you can redo your stitches without damaging the fabric.

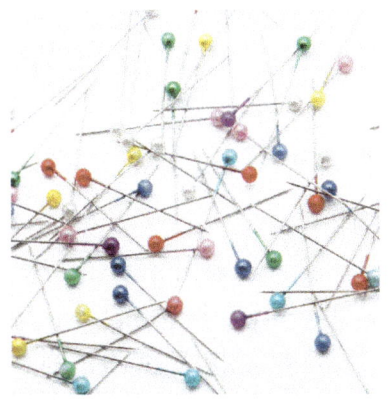

PINS

Also called dressmaker pins and all-purpose pins, straight pins are made of stainless steel and are used to nail different fabrics. They can come with round or flatheads. If you're a beginner, round head pins are easier to handle.

NEEDLE THREADER

Threading the tiny eye of a needle can be a daunting task even for experienced hobbyists. To save time, it's best to get a needle threader to help you thread needles easily. This is a metal gadget that comes with a loop of thread that goes through the needle's eye. Place the wire in the loop and remove it. Once pulled back, the thread will go inside the eye.

SHEARS

Shears are the best cutting tools for sewing. They are different from scissors because they have asymmetrical handle sizes, thus providing more leverage when you use them to cut fabric. The handles are also bent upward, so the fabric lies flat on the table when cutting. Never use shears to cut paper because it dulls them.

THIMBLE

A thimble is a small metal cup that fits over your fingertips. Its primary function is to protect the fingers that push the needle when hand sewing so that they don't get pricked or bruised over time. People often use this when working with heavy fabrics.

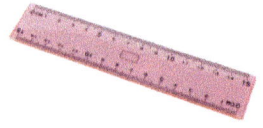

GRIDDED RULER

A clear plastic rule is essential for your sewing kit as it allows you to make a straight line on the fabric.

SHARPENER

OF COURSE, you need a sharpener to make sure your pencils stay in perfect shape, literally and figuratively. A regular pencil sharpener will do that.

TAPE MEASURE

Sewing requires you to take the necessary measurements; therefore, it's essential to include a measuring tool in your kit. Tape measures often have a total length of 60 inches. Be sure to choose one with imperial measurements on one side and the metric equivalent on the other.

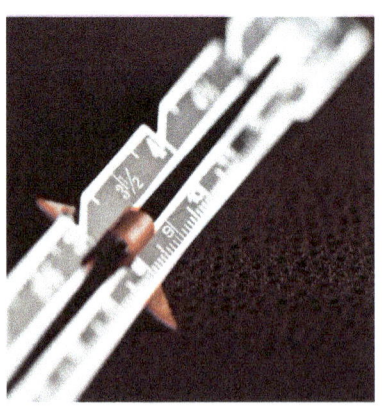

STITCHING GAUGE RULER

A seam gauge is a 5-inch-long ruler with a sliding indicator that runs the entire length of the ruler. It lets you make consistent seam allowances, so you don't run out of fabric while sewing.

Fabric markers

It's important to transfer your patterns onto the fabric, and this can be achieved by using fabric markers. You can purchase fabric markers from your local haberdashery store. Make sure you don't replace them with a pen or pencil because the ink may not easily wash off the fabric.

ROTARY cutter

Rotary cutters will help you cut fabric and thread precisely as you want and help you create straight edges. These are best used for long slices and curves.

Tailor

A seam ripper is an inexpensive little tool that

comes in handy when you need to reverse your mistakes. As the name suggests, if you see seams in what you're doing, you can undo them with this.

Ironing board

A regular-sized one will do, but keep in mind that it is available in other sizes as well. Besides being useful for your projects, you know you can use one in your everyday life too!

Folding pen

Folding pens make it easy to create precise folds in the fabric. They also keep pleats sharp and in place, so you won't risk burning your fingers trying to hold the hem in place while ironing.

IRON STEAM

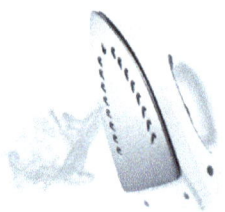

Choose a reliable brand of iron that heats evenly and has various steam settings to suit the range of fabric types you might use.

Cloth pressing

A pressing cloth will prevent unnecessary heating, especially on sensitive clothes or fabrics, and protect the quality of your projects.

Mini iron

This is designed for smaller, lighter types of fabric that can't handle too much heat.

Nosepiece pressing

Nosepiece pressing makes it easier to iron those hard-to-reach edges and curved, ohm seams.

Don't Miss it in Your Special Sewing Kit

While hand sewing is a great way to create exciting projects, there are times when machine sewing is better. This is especially true if you want to do complicated projects in a short amount of time. Creating a machine sewing kit is easy. In addition to the basic materials and tools mentioned above, the following are the other things you need for your machine sewing kit.

Sewing Machine

You need a sewing machine, of course. If you are a beginner, choose a sewing machine that has the basic features. You need a decent but reliable machine that you can use to develop your sewing skills. Don't be persuaded by the seller to get an expensive machine that comes with 1,000 stitches. When choosing a sewing machine, think about what you want to do. Do you want to do simple sewing or quilting? Determining your sewing goals can help you decide what kind of sewing machine you need.

Brush

GRANDMA'S BASICS SEWING

A small brush allows you to clean the nooks and crannies of your sewing machine. Remember that dust or lint can jam up the inner workings of the machine.

PRESSER FOOT

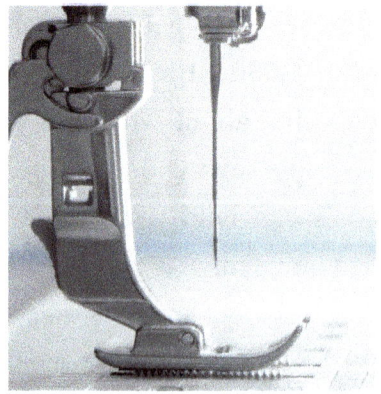

The presser foot holds the fabric firmly as the

needle moves in and out of the fabric. The presser foot keeps the fabric stable so you can sew evenly on it.

BOBBINS

A sewing machine works because the top and bottom threads intertwine with each other. While the top thread is on the spindle, the bottom thread is in the bobbin. When you buy a sewing machine, it usually provides three bobbins, but it's best if you keep several bobbins on hand, so you don't have to unravel a bobbin every time you use a new color of thread.

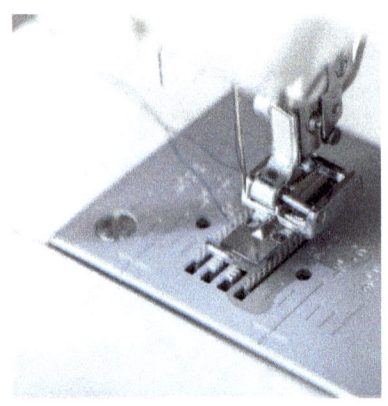

ZIPPER FOOT

A zipper foot is an essential tool that allows you to put a zipper in your sewing project. It is also used in inserting piping and cables if you are making home decorations like curtains or seat covers.

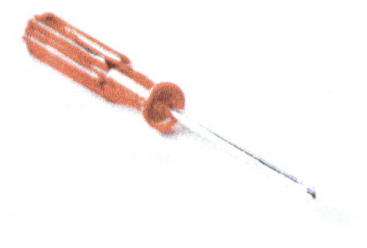

SCREWDRIVER

A screwdriver is an essential tool when using a sewing machine. You need to use it to loosen or tighten the screw that holds the machine's needle in place.

Storage and Fabric

Although sewing supplies don't take up a lot of space, that's precisely why they can easily get lost. There's nothing more frustrating than not finding an object when you need it most. Storage solutions come in many different sizes and budgets. Therefore, starting small isn't such a bad idea.

A multi-storage box with mini clear drawers is always handy for storing small stuff. A pigeon keeps your needles in place because the last thing you want is a minefield of needles in your home.

ONCE THE SEWING frenzy gets a hold of you, fabrics will start piling up in your home. That's when you'll want to have a clear overview of your fabrics. For this, you can simply fold your fabrics and place them vertically in inboxes. This way, you know exactly what fabrics you have, and you don't have to make a huge mess while trying to pull out a particular piece.

YOU CAN STORE your fabrics by whatever category

makes the most sense to you. It can be by color, type (see "Fabrics"), or size.

Silky fabrics don't like to stay neatly folded, but an elastic band can tame them.

Using the suitable fabric is very important for sewing. Buying them can also be addictive. However, before you stock up on fabric, make sure you know how to choose the suitable fabric to work with. This section will discuss tips on how to select the suitable fabric for your sewing projects.

You will realize that there are hundreds of fabrics to choose from. If you are a beginner in sewing, selecting the suitable fabric to work with is essential. Below is a list of the different types of fabrics used.

Polyester

Synthetic fabrics are lightweight and crease-resistant. They are also fairly inexpensive, which makes them, beautiful fabrics for beginners.

Choosing the suitable fabric can be overwhelming for beginners. To begin with, it's essential to select a fabric to practice your sewing skills on, so starting with a relatively cheaper fabric is the best choice. Aside from this factor, below are the other things you need to consider when choosing the suitable fabric.

Choose fabrics because they won't slip or stretch when sewn. These include cotton or linen. Avoid knitted fabrics because they are challenging to work with.

Select fabrics with simple colors and small prints. Avoid fabrics that have large patterns or stripes because they are tough to stretch.

Avoid heavy fabrics because they are difficult to manipulate. Heavy fabrics include denim and corduroy.

Deciding which fabric you need to purchase is fundamental. However, fabric shopping can become a daunting task. The following are the things you need to do when shopping for fabrics.

Unroll the fabric just a bit to see how it drapes. Try to see how it feels. Does it feel smooth or scratchy? Choose fabrics that have a good drape.

Look at the fabric label and try to find out the fiber content and care instructions. If you think the fabric is too high maintenance, move on to the next one.

Fabrics come in a variety of widths, including 60 inches and 45 inches. Be sure to purchase the fabric your pattern needs.

When purchasing fabrics, you must take your time in choosing the right ones for your sewing projects.

Cotton

Cotton is considered the most versatile fabric and is used to make shirts, skirts, bags, and all kinds of sewing projects. It is also quite cheaper than other fabrics.

Wool

Wool fabric is knitted or woven. It is made into

dresses, elegant skirts, pants, and coats. It tends to be expensive.

Linen

Linen is a woven fabric that has different weights. It creases a lot, which makes it a bit difficult to work with. It is used to make different types of sundresses and other summer clothes because of its lightweight feel.

Cotton Jersey

A machine knits cotton jersey from fine cotton fibers. It has a stretchy characteristic and is also very comfortable to wear. Unfortunately, the cotton jersey is not very easy for beginners to sewing.

Silk

Silk is an expensive woven fabric and is shiny and has slippery characteristics. It is used to make luxury clothing and is therefore very expensive. Because of its slipperiness, it can be quite tricky to sew silk.

BASIC SEWING PATTERNS

Now that you know what you need to have on hand, it's time for you to learn about the basic stitches!

Choosing Your Pattern

Creating a new pattern depends to a large extent on one's creativity and knack for innovation. They can be very simple, involving few turns and twists, or extremely complex and highly advanced at the same time.

As a beginner, you should start with a pattern that does not need a cocktail of too many skills at a single time. Going with a complex pattern before getting versed with the basics might end you up frustrated and bored.

Most people prefer to begin with letters or numbers as patterns, for example, A, Z, C, 8, 5, and so on. Rather than choosing your pattern based on the parameters like "quick" and "easy," it might be beneficial if you make the selection on the basis of what skills, or to be more accurate, how many skills the work is going to employ at the very first instance.

Taking up a single concept at a time will help you in understanding the intricacies in a much better way. For example, in my personal choice, I would definitely not take up a pattern with buttonholes, gathering, zippers, darts and difficult collars if I'm encountering it for the first time. Always move on to another skill only after you have mastered the first one, otherwise, you would lose all the fun of sewing.

Pattern selection is not an exercise that can be accomplished in isolation; it goes along with fabric selection. One should avoid purchasing the fabric unless the pattern has been finalized.

For a beginner, the first project should be a non-clothing one as clothing projects need an additional headache—that of fitting—which may be an over-burden for the first-timer. In the first project, you should just concern yourself with getting familiarity with the machine, with various stitches and cutting techniques, learning the methods to guide your fabric through the machine, and most importantly, learning to sew in a straight line

Sewing Seams

THE FIRST THING you have to know about working on seams is that you can use thread in two ways: Single or Double threading. Here's how:

Single Threading. Once you've inserted the thread into the eye, pull it out and make sure that it's only a few inches away from the end of the needle. Cut the thread into the length that you like, knot it and begin sewing.

Double Threading. Insert the thread through the eye of the needle, then double it up to help you get a thicker kind of thread. Let the end of the thread meet up with the spooled thread so that you'll get two tail ends. Knot these two ends together and then start sewing the fabric with the doubled thread.

There are three knots that you can make when you're trying to sew seams. You might not have to use all of them at once. Check out the guide below for details.

First Knot. If you have used double threading, make sure that you cut the thread that you can see below the needle's eye to get a standard knot together with two tails.

Second Knot. This can be used for both single and double threading. First, hold the thread in one hand and the needle in the other. Then, pull the thread after looping it in a counterclockwise manner to form the start of a knot. As you move the thread to the fabric, make sure that you tighten it and keep the knot in place with one or two fingers.

Third Knot. To do the third knot, you need to have some stitches on the wrong side of the cloth. Form a loop by slipping the needle under the stitch and then pull to tighten it. Do this at least two to three times to secure the knot and you're set.

Now that you have formed a knot, it's time to start stitching. First, we will discuss two basic stitches: the basting stitch and the running stitch. Don't forget to thread your needle and form a knot before beginning.

Basting Stitch. Basting is a loose, temporary stitch used to hold the layers of your fabric together while you sew. It can be easily removed with a seam ripper once you are finished. To create the basting stitch, make around ¼" to ½" long stitches to whatever you want to seam.

Running Stitch. The running stitch is a simple stitch commonly used in sewing. It is similar in technique to the basting stitch, but the stitches are placed closer together as they are intended to be permanent. Start stitching from where you first inserted the thread and then stitch the length of the seam you are sewing by passing the needle in and out of the fabric. Keep "running" until you need to.

Backstitching

Now, it's time to do some backstitches. Backstitching is a simple and strong stitch that will make your projects seem as if they were done with the help of a machine.

To backstitch, begin by threading your needle and knotting the end of the thread. Insert the needle into the wrong side of the fabric, then pull until you reach the knot you have made earlier.

Start making small stitches from the knot all the way to the left or right. When you reach your starting position at the wrong side of the fabric, stitch to a position that's one stitch wider than the last. Remember that it's up to you to keep the stitches as close or wide as possible. Spacing will always depend on you, so think about what kind of spacing you want.

Slip stitching

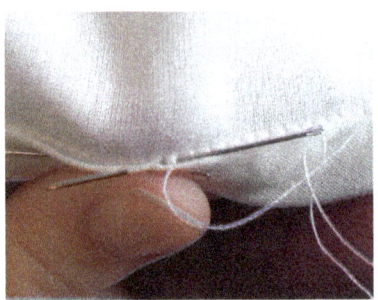

SLIP stitching is a bit more complicated, but you will easily master it after some practice. Slip stitching allows you to create stitches that look almost invisible so that your projects end up looking flawless.

To do slip stitches, cut a small piece of cloth and then press it after folding it in half. Open the cloth and fold it so that both sides will be turned to the centerline. Fold it again along the centerline, then double thread your needle by inserting the thread through the eye of the needle and then double it up to help you get a thicker kind of thread. Let the end of the thread meet up with the spooled thread so that you have two tail ends. Knot these two ends together and then start sewing the fabric with the doubled thread.

Then, make a knot by pulling the needle atop the cloth, making sure to stay close to the edge of the folded cloth. Keep pulling until you catch the knot and then move all the way down to the final fold of the cloth at the bottom. Stick the needle into the creased part of the cloth and push it until you only see about ¼ inch of it and then pull the thread some more. Push horizontally and repeat the process all the way to the end.

Once you reach the end, start making small stitches opposite the long fold of the cloth. Pull the thread until you have a small loop and then put the needle in twice more. Form a knot by pulling the thread and repeat once more to fully tighten it.

Decorative Stitches

Decorative stitches are aesthetically pleasing stitches that will give your project that extra flair.

Whip Stitch. To do whip stitches, fold a piece of cloth in half and pin it to keep it from shifting. Insert the needle on the top fold after opening it and make sure that the needle comes through the back all the way to the front. Then, make stitches that make your next couple of stitches in the same level as your first couple of stitches. End it with blanket stitches which you'll learn about below.

Blanket Stitch. To make blanket stitches, go to the front end of the fabric and pull the needle from there. Then, thread the needle diagonally so you can make diagonal stitches on the wrong side of the fabric. Keep pulling as you make diagonal stitches and then end where you see the largest kind of diagonal stitch.

Now, loop your needle to the diagonal and pull at a 90º angle on the stitch. Continue to sew more diagonal stitches. Pull some more until needed.

To end the stitches, loop the needle to the vertical side of the fabric and make another loop. Then insert the needle there at least thrice and end the stitch with a knot.

French Seams

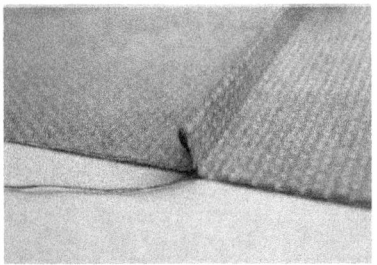

FRENCH SEAMS WILL PROVE to be extremely useful if you're the type who wants to create your own home decors, totes, purses and the like. They may seem complicated at first, but you can learn how to make them—and you'll learn how here!

1. The easiest trick is to make at least 1/8 to ¼ allowances on the seam so you don't waste time cutting off the excess fabric. This will also make your projects look coherent. Here's a step-by-step process to help you understand it better.
2. Cut two pieces of cloth and then place them on top of each other, making sure that the wrong sides are facing each other.
3. Start from the right edge of the fabric and sew at least 1/8 inch of seam.
4. Then, lay the fabric open and finger press the seam so that it lays flat.

5. Next, fold the fabric and start sewing again, making sure that the right edge is visible.
6. Use at least ¼ inch of allowance while sewing, and finish the entire length of the seam.
7. Use an iron to press down on the fabric, starting from the opposite side all the way to the front. Sewing the allowance of the seam will provide you with a flat and nicely done project.

Sewing Buttons

AND OF COURSE, there are times when you have to sew buttons on the projects that you are making. Here is a simple guide to help you learn how.

Button Types

There are two common types of buttons that you can use:

- Shank Buttons. Shank buttons are buttons that do not have holes on top of them. However, they have a hollow lump on the back so that they can be threaded. These buttons are often used for coats and dresses.
- Flat Buttons. Flat buttons are the buttons you see on most types of clothing, especially dress shirts. They typically have 2 to 4 holes on them.

What You Need:

Here are the items you need in order to sew on a button:

- Buttons
- 8 inches of thread that has been doubled
- Fabric marking pen or pencil
- Needle

How to Do It:

1. When sewing a shank button: mark the spot where you want to attach the button. Bring your threaded needle up through the fabric at

the spot you have marked and pass it through the loop on the back of the button.
2. Pull the thread so that the button sits snugly against the fabric
3. Secure the shank button by passing the needle up through the fabric and through the back of the button 8-10 times.
4. Then, knot the thread on the wrong side of the fabric a few times to anchor the button and cut off the excess thread.
5. When sewing a flat button; make sure that again, you mark the spot where you want the button to be.
6. Then loop your needle on the side of the fabric right next to the spot that you have marked.

1. Thread the needle up through one of the

buttonholes and then back down through the other buttonhole and through the fabric. Pull the thread tightly so that the button sits against the fabric and continue looping the needle through the buttonholes to anchor it securely to the fabric.

That's it—you're ready to go!

Chapter 6: Are You Ready to Sew? Let's Start Together!

IF THIS IS your first time with a machine, it will be somewhat daunting in the beginning. The best advice I can give you is to relax and have a lot of fun. You are not going to be turning out professional-looking garments the first time, so grab some old bits of material, something cheap that is not slippery—cotton or calico perhaps—and get some brightly colored thread.

This is so you can see your stitches and monitor how well you are doing.

Threading Your Machine

Before you begin working on any sort of project, you'll need to know how to thread your machine. I'll show you in pictures, but it'll be up to you to practice it several times. Every machine will be different, but to help you get a better understanding of how the process works, I can show you the pictures of how threading your machine will most likely be.

To start threading your machine, we'll start first with your thread. Place a spool of thread on the spindle at the top of your machine. Keep it in place by putting a spool holder over the top of it. A spool holder is a plastic cap that will fit snugly onto your spindle, clamping right over your spool. You can see it in the picture below; it looks like a little hat:

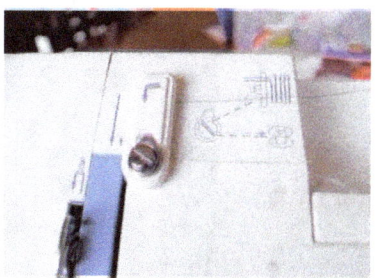

TAKE the thread off your spindle and get ready to start threading. On the top of your machine, you'll see a few images like the following picture:

Those images will be your machine's personal guide to threading your machine. Follow the guide. Once you have this portion figured out, you'll usually have to pull the thread down into the machine, like in the next picture:

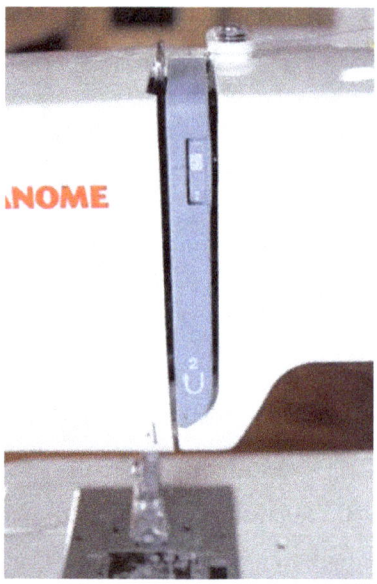

THIS LOOP IS CALLED the "thread take-up lever." You'll loop your thread around the bottom, bringing it up. Your machine will have a metal piece that will take hold of the thread when you bring it up. Weave it through and then the thread will come back down again. When you bring it down, you should use your machine's needle threader to help you get the string into the needle.

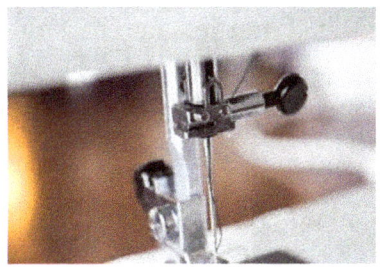

Your needle has been successfully threaded. But that's just the first part. In order to complete the threading, you'll need to put it in your bobbin. Make sure it's been wound first, as in the thread has been placed on it. You need a wound bobbin before you thread your machine. Next to your spindle for the spool, you'll see the following piece of metal:

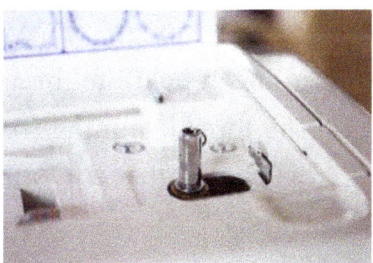

This is the bobbin winder. Notice how the metal has space so it can be pushed to the right and then back to the left? When it's in the correct spot for winding bobbins, your machine will not sew and pressing on the pedal will engage the bobbin winder.

To thread your bobbin, simply place your bobbin spool onto the metal pole. If you have fine eyesight, you should see in this picture a little piece of metal sticking out to the right of the bobbin winder. This metal will hold your bobbin in place.

Now, from your spool, take the free thread and wrap it around your bobbin a couple of times. I like to simply hold it while the bobbin spins, but many machines have a way to lock the loose thread into place, so you don't have to hold it. Do what works best for you. Once your thread has been securely attached to your bobbin, and the bobbin winder has been engaged by pushing the bobbin winder into the "on" position, use the foot pedal to wind that baby up!

Try not to go too fast though, or your bobbin will not thread evenly. You can help the threading along by gently pushing on the thread running from your spool to the bobbin if it begins to pile up in one place for too long without moving on.

Once your bobbin is nice and full, push the winder back into the "off" position. Remember, if your bobbin is "on," your machine will not sew, but the winder will move when the pedal is pressed.

Now you're ready to put your bobbin into place. To get the bobbin to your machine, take off the bobbin cover (usually a clear plastic almost-square piece). Reference the picture below:

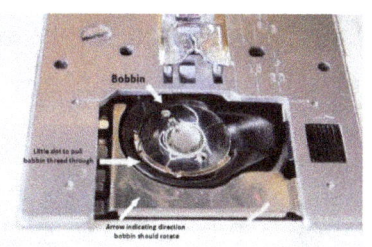

YOUR BOBBIN COVER will fit right over this section of your machine, which is right beneath your footer. If your machine doesn't look anything like this, you'll need to consult your manual. Once your bobbin is in place, make sure you leave a piece of thread out, threaded through the thin slot. It is perfectly fine to leave the loose strand out while you work; in fact, it's necessary.

Put the cover back over your bobbin and now you're ready to get sewing! Grab a piece of fabric (anything you can toss in the trash will do), pull up a chair with some back support and read on to learn about sewing a straight line!

How to Prepare the Fabric

Now that you know the basic sewing stitches, you

need to know how to prepare your fabric before you start sewing. There is more to sewing than just putting your thread and needle on the fabric. You need to avoid cutting through your fabric at once. You need to prepare your fabric so that you will be able to successfully make your sewing projects. Below are the things you need to do to prepare the fabric.

Pre-Shrink the Fabric

When you buy a piece of fabric, make sure you know about the care directions. These are usually found on the end of the fabric. Before sewing, it is important that all the elements of a particular project should be pre-shrunk, and this includes the zipper, interfacing and even the lining. To pre-shrink the fabric, fill a tub or basin with warm water and soak your fabric for a few seconds. Pre-shrinking the fabric ensures that the amount of fabric you use is just enough.

To find out if your fabric shrinks, cut a precise 2" square piece off your fabric and wet it with warm water. Press it with a steam iron. Draw a 2" square on a piece of paper and lay your dry fabric swatch over it. If it fills the entire box, then the fabric did not shrink. This test will save you a lot of time in figuring out whether your fabric will shrink or not.

If the fabric is colored, it may bleed a lot, so it is important to check for colorfastness. To do this, you need to wash the fabric with a scrap of cotton fabric. If the white fabric comes out with a tint of color, then you can conclude that your fabric bleeds. You can control the bleeding of your fabric by washing it with three tablespoons of vinegar to help set the color. It is important that you set the colors on your fabric, especially if your project calls for two or three types of fabric. For fabrics that require dry-cleaning, you can steam shrink them by dampening the fabric and steam pressing it on the wrong side until it dries. Once it is dry, remove the creases from the fabric. Removing the creases ensures that the shapes, as well as sizes of the pattern that you cut, are accurate.

How to Check the Grain of the Fabric

The grain refers to the direction in which the thread runs. When sewing different fabrics, it is important that the lengthwise and crosswise threads meet at the appropriate angles. If you sew on different threads, the final product will end up twisted or will hang crookedly.

It is important to take note that all types of woven fabrics have crosswise and lengthwise grains and both run perpendicular to each other. If you are sewing a garment, the lengthwise grain should run vertically from the shoulders to the hem. If you are sewing drapes or curtains, you need to run the grain from top to bottom.

Prepare the Pattern

When sewing fabrics, you need to use patterns to be

able to successfully create the final project. To prepare your fabric for pattern making, follow the steps below:

1. Give your pattern a press if it is folded or has wrinkles to help with accurate cutting.
2. Find a long table and wipe it down. Make sure it is free from any bumps that may obstruct you from laying out your pattern.
3. Fold your fabric in half lengthwise with all the right sides together, thus matching the two selvedges. They are the firmly woven border along the lengthwise edges. Folding the fabric makes it easier to cut it into two of the same piece at once. Before you fold the fabric, make sure the print is right-side up.
4. Smooth the fabric to make the sides as flat as possible. If the fabric is longer than the table, lay out as much of it as you can while the other end is rolled neatly. By doing so, you can cut the pieces one at a time and unroll more as you go.
5. Place the pattern on top of the fabric. If you want to utilize all of your fabric, then you can arrange the fabric fold as long as the selvedges remain precisely parallel with one another.
6. Follow the pattern guide sheet so that you can determine where to put all the pattern

pieces. Secure the patterns with pins and you are ready for cutting.

How to Cut the Fabric

Once you have prepared the pattern, it is time to cut through your garment. This procedure requires you to be accurate. It is very important for all the seams to go together, and thus cutting with the grain is necessary. This section will provide you tips on how to cut fabrics properly so that you can sew better.

1. Use a cutting mat with a grid to help you cut your fabric precisely.
2. Make sure that you measure multiple spots on the entire grain line.
3. It is also important that all pattern pieces are laid correctly.
4. Place pins in the fabric. Leave a 1" allowance after the pattern. Place the pins within the allowance to secure the fabric in place.
5. Cut using very sharp scissors, as the seams of the hemline line up more easily if you use sharp scissors.
6. Cut along the allowance. If you feel like you cannot cut around the pins, use a rotary cutter instead. Using a rotary cutter can reduce the fraying of the edges of the fabric.

Selecting a Pattern

Ready-made patterns found in stores can be intimidating, but don't worry; you can learn to navigate them.

First of all, choose a pattern that is labeled "easy." Have a look at the front page. The sketch version of the garment will give you an idea of the front and back look.

Next, you will see the table of measurements on the back. Note that the measurements are usually smaller than ready-made garments you find in stores, so in order to avoid ending up with a garment that is too small, double-check your body measurements and cut a little bit bigger than the pattern suggests.

You will see a list of pieces that you need to cut out. For example:

- Front
- Back
- Sleeve
- Pocket

Below that will be a list of items called "notions." Notions are any supplies other than fabric, such as buttons, lining, straps and threads.

Pattern Layout

As you open the envelope, you will find all the pieces marked with their corresponding numbers. You will also see multiple dotted lines. These mark the different sizes, so make sure you cut the size that you need. Along these lines, you will come across small triangles. These are notches that you will eventually need to cut out.

Cut out all the pieces in their biggest form.

Once you decide which size fits you, lay your fabric flat on an even surface. The fabric should lay straight, not diagonal. Next, pin the pattern pieces on the fabric. Cut out to the right size with long and firm cuts.

Here are the most common pattern markings and their functions:

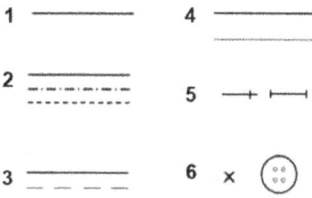

1. Cutting Line
2. Lines corresponding to different sizes
3. Seam allowance
4. Hemline
5. Buttonholes
6. Button placement

MARKING

Once you have cut out your pieces, it is wise to mark important lines and points such as darts or buttonholes from the paper onto the fabric. One easy method is to use a fabric pen. Make a tiny hole in the paper to mark it onto the fabric. Another way is to make some hand stitches through the paper and fabric. Once you are done marking this way, you can gently tear off the paper. The stitches will remain in place on the fabric.

Sewing a Seam

There are four main seams that serve different purposes:

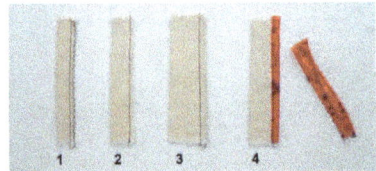

Zigzag Seam

A zigzag seam is a good alternative to the serger seam. A serger or overlock machine is a separate machine that trims and finishes the raw edges of a garment while simultaneously sewing the pieces together. Sergers are usually more expensive than regular sewing machines, so unless you are very serious about sewing, the zigzag will do the job. After stitching the pieces together, set the machine on a zigzag stitch and sew along the edge.

Stitch and Pink Seam

Pinking shears are wonderful when it comes to finishing raw edges. The zigzag shape of the scissors prevents the fabric from fraying too much. This seam is suitable for most fabrics.

French Seam

A French seam is suitable for delicate fabrics and classy outfits that should look good both on the right side as well as on the wrong side. For this seam, the seam allowance is twice as wide as a normal seam. The seam is stitched on the right side of the garment first, then turned inside out, pressed and stitched again.

Hong Kong Seam

A more elaborate but elegant-looking finish is done with a Hong Kong seam. Here, the edges are enclosed in bias tape. It is obviously more time-consuming, but the results are well worth it. The Hong Kong seam gives a professional look and provides more structure due to its thickness.

Threading and Tension

Most sewing machines have a similar threading system. The correct threading is essential; otherwise, the machine will not be able to stitch properly, or the thread might break while stitching.

GRANDMA'S BASICS SEWING

1. The sewing machine may have markings to show you the steps you need to follow. First, place the thread spool onto the shaft.

1. Then bring it along with the marked areas.

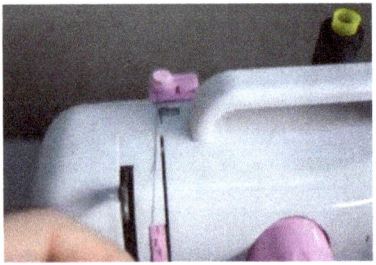

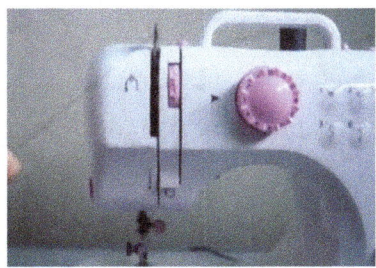

1. Lastly, insert the thread through the needle. Some advanced sewing machines can do this with the push of a button.

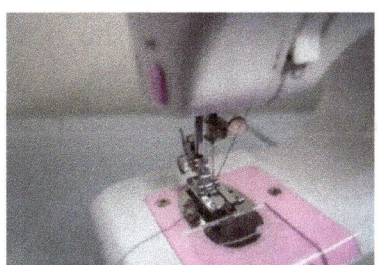

THREADING the Bobbin

There are plastic bobbins and metal bobbins. Many sewing machines have a magnet in the bobbin hole to keep the metal bobbins in place. Test out whether your sewing machine has a magnetic bobbing hole by swiping a magnet or a small metal item on the area. Note that plastic bobbins are not as efficient on a magnetic bobbin hole.

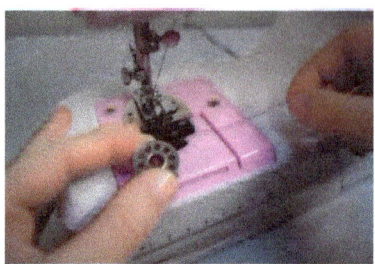

TO GET the thread out from the bottom onto the surface, align the bobbin with the thread unraveling clockwise. Let a few inches of thread stick out. Lower the needle by turning the wheel toward you. The needle will pull out the lower thread.

BRING the two threads underneath the presser foot, allowing a good 4" of thread to stick out. Then place your piece of fabric underneath and lower the foot.

Tension

Tension is the pulling strength between the upper and lower threads. There is a button or small wheel with which you can control the tension. In most cases, you will use a tension of 3-4. The higher the number, the tighter the upper thread will be. For low tension, dial in a lower number.

The tension adjustment depends on what type of fabric you use. Every time you start using a new type of fabric, make a few stitches on a scrap to recalibrate the tension. Generally, the thicker the fabric, the higher the tension required.

Signs of Mismatched Tension

If the tension does not match the thickness of the fabric, the error will be obvious. Either the threads will be so tense that they gather the fabric, or the threads will be too loose and won't be able to keep the fabrics together. In other cases, the upper thread could simply snap because of high tension.

If this happens, simply dial the tension wheel forward or back and make some stitches until you find the right position. Knowing intuitively what tension you need requires some experience, so don't worry if you get it wrong.

Start Stitching

First, make sure your machine is set on basic stitch and you have threaded it properly. You should have around 4 inches of spare thread pulled out so that it can't unthread from the machine. Another thing that will help is if you hold the thread for the first couple of stitches.

Put the fabric underneath the presser foot, making sure the bit you want to stitch is at the front of the machine. Lower the presser foot to hold the fabric in place. This is an easy thing to forget, but you'll only do it a few times after your stitches run wild! Make it your mantra for a while— "lower the presser foot" —and keep on repeating it until you've mastered it.

The upper thread should be on top of the fabric but underneath the presser foot, while the lower thread from the bobbin should be underneath the fabric. Both of the threads should stick out to the back, so you are not sewing over them and getting them knotted up.

Before you begin any new line, check that you have

lifted the needle up as high as it will go. This will help to prevent any of the frustrations of the thread from getting stuck or unraveling.

Turn on your machine. Lightly put both hands on the fabric on either side of the presser foot. This is to help guide it while sewing. Do not push or pull it and keep your fingers out of the way of the needle—it will hurt! Lower your foot gently onto the pedal and start stitching.

Get lots of practice at this because it's the only way to learn how to guide the fabric and keep your stitching straight and neat.

Once you've got the hang of it, you can start looking at changing your speed. Most machines will have a speed setting button so you can slow it down or speed it up as you see fit. If your machine is one that does not have a speed setting, you will need to learn how to control the speed through the pressure you put on the pedal.

How to Use the Hand Wheel

If you want to sew very slowly or you want to be able to move by just a stitch or two at a time for precision sewing, you can use the handwheel. Turn it toward you to manually do what the pedal does. You can use the handwheel to make your first stitch if you like to make sure the thread doesn't unravel or loosen and to ensure the needle goes where you want it. This is great for controlling the amount the needle moves through the fabric. I use it all the time for finishing off, turning corners, or for precision when doing topstitching.

Cut Loose

When you have finished your stitching, raise the presser foot so you can pull the fabric out slightly. Don't forget to raise your needle as well! You can do this with the handwheel if you like; just raise the needle enough to make the thread give a little and you can move the fabric. Then, snip off the threads with small sharp scissors.

Some machines have a handy little blade on the side you can use to snip it off in one quick move, but you will need to check the manual for directions on how to use it.

Securing the Stitches

When you start sewing properly, i.e., not during a practice run, you will want to start securing your stitches so they can't come undone. There are two ways to do this:

Hold the reverse stitch lever on the machine so you sew backward a few stitches over the end of the stitches —this is known as "back tacking." Stitch forward again and snip the threads. This is probably the way you will do it most of the time.

If you have already sewn off the end of the fabric, simply tie the thread ends together into a double knot and snip off the ends. You would usually do this when you are sewing darts or in other tricky little spots where you don't want bulky reverse stitching.

Stitching a Straight Line

Once you have the hang of stitching with the machine, it is time to start learning how to stitch in a straight line. To begin, use a ruler and draw a straight line on the fabric. You can use the needle plate guidelines as well—these will tell you how far the needle is from the edge of the fabric. Take some time to learn how the fabric goes through the machine and how to control it until you are satisfied and you can sew in a straight line.

Stitching a Curved Line

When you can sew in a straight line, have a go at sewing in curves. Again, draw a line on your fabric, a nice wavy one, but keep the curves large for now until you have the hang of it. Put the fabric onto the machine and make sure the presser foot is in line with the first part of the curve.

When you start to sew, gently guide the fabric with your hands and make sure the presser foot remains in line with the upcoming curve. Go slowly; stop as many times as you need to keep up with the curves. This will take practice, so keep going until you are certain your stitching is following the line of your curves.

One thing you might find with curves is that you need to snip the fabric to keep these curves nice and flat. If you are sewing a curved seam, for example, when you turn the item the right way out, there may be areas that are puckered. Snipping the fabric will prevent this from happening.

Turning the Corner

Start by drawing a right angle on your fabric. Get the fabric into the machine and start stitching along the line until you get to the corner. At the point of the corner, the needle must be pushed down through your fabric—if it isn't going, use the handwheel to help it. Raise the presser foot when the needle is in the right place, turn the fabric so the next straight line is in front of you and check that it is parallel to the needle plate guidelines. Put the presser foot back down and continue stitching.

CONCLUSIONS

Sewing has become a worldwide art, where millions of customers and individual consumers are served each day, with different kinds of products, using sewing techniques. Sewing is no more a manual and traditional task. It has become a complete digital and computerized technique. This is because of different kinds of machines and tools that are based on different kinds of sophisticated technology. With this advancement, sewing has become a passion for several people around the globe. We have written this book, keeping in mind the interest of several our readers.

All the types of techniques are elaborately discussed so that the readers can easily choose the appropriate technique, according to the type of fabric and the pattern to be made. We hope that we have become successful in elaborating all the important issues to our

CONCLUSIONS

readers, so that the manuscript can serve as the complete guide to the sewing practice.

Now, new and enhanced designs and patterns have been used in order to give advanced looks to outfits. Extra time can be utilized in creating something beautiful so it is a good activity for spending leisure time. Sewing can be used for earning revenue also. Family income could be supplemented by sewing. It also can be adopted as small or medium-term businesses. There is a tremendous style for different dresses. Simple to complex projects can be handled with this art. In fact, sewing is the basis for every stylish item.

www.ingramcontent.com/pod-product-compliance
Lightning Source LLC
Chambersburg PA
CBHW062146100526
44589CB00014B/1697